KALIMBA SONGBOOK

Thomas Balinger
Lena Eckhoff

50 EASY CLASSIC SONGS

**10 and 17 key
Kalimba
in C**

Thomas Balinger, Lena Eckhoff
Kalimba Songbook, 50 Easy Classic Songs

© 2019

Revised edition 2020-01

ISBN: 9781072334903

Preface

Hello and welcome to this kalimba songbook!
This book is written for the beginning player, featuring easy arrangements of popular songs and large notation plus an extra line of kalimba tablature to make playing these songs as easy as possible (more on kalimba tablature on p. 10).

With the exception of *Aura Lee* (p.44), all songs in this book can be played on either a 10 key or a 17 key kalimba (mbira, marimba) in C tuning.

We included short sections on tuning your kalimba, kalimba care and the playing basics to get you playing as fast as possible. Last not least, there's a short introduction to the basics of reading music at the end of the book.

Wishing you lots of fun with this great little instrument,
Lena Eckhoff, Thomas Balinger

Contents

Songs

Kalimba models

There are dozens of kalimba models, with the main difference being the tuning of the instrument and the number of keys (tines). All songs in this book have been arranged for the most commonly played 10 and 17 tine models tuned to C.

Kalimba (17 key model)

Kalimba (10 key model)

Holding and playing your kalimba

Use the thumbs of both hands to play the keys of the instrument while holding it with your remaining fingers. Normally, the right hand thumb plays the keys to the right of the longest key (including the longest key itself) while the left hand thumb plays those on the left side.
Play the keys with the fleshy part of your thumb(s) or use the nail for a crisper sound with more treble and definition.
You can open and close the little holes on the back of the instrument to create sound effects.
Some players prefer to lay the instrument on a table or another flat surface for higher volume.
Experiment and see what you like.

Take a look at the playing position pictured above and you'll see why the kalimba is sometimes called **thumb piano**.

Kalimba care and maintenance

Your kalimba doesn't need much in the care department. Use the bag or case it came in to store it when not playing and clean its surface from time to time with a soft cloth and some guitar polish (or violin oil). Like all wooden instruments, your kalimba doesn't like very high (or very low) humidity and sudden temperature changes.

Kalimba tuning

Though your kalimba doesn't need to be tuned as often as a guitar or a violin, there will come a moment it needs to be tuned. To properly tune your kalimba you'll need two things:

1. An electronic tuner, available at your local music dealer or on the internet. Shop for a chromatic model. A guitar or ukulele tuner won't do because it can't recognize all the notes of your kalimba. You can also download a tuner app to your smartphone.

2. The tuning tool (or some similar small hammer) that came with your kalimba.

And here's how its done: Use your tuner to check the pitch of the tine(s) that are out of tune. The tuner will tell you if the tine's pitch is too low or too high.

Tine pitch to high: use the tuning tool to move the respective tine slightly in the direction of the soundhole.

Tine pitch to low: use the tuning tool to move the respective tine slightly in the other direction (away from the soundhole).

Work with very small and deliberate action of the tuning tool and never use excessive force!
Hint: When tuning my kalimba, I like to protect its top with a small piece of cloth (e.g. a kitchen towel), to avoid scratching or damaging the instrument's top with the tuning tool.

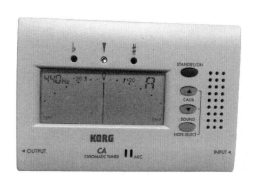

Chromatic tuner

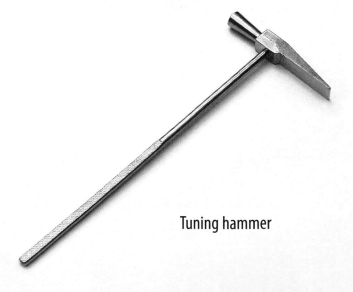

Tuning hammer

Notes & stickers

Your kalimba probably came with a small assortment of adhesive stickers to fit to your instrument. These are meant to help you find your way around the instrument more easily. Fix them as in the graphics below so you can always find the right notes at a glance.

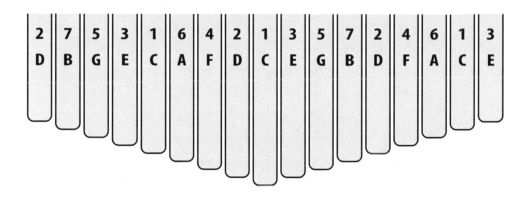

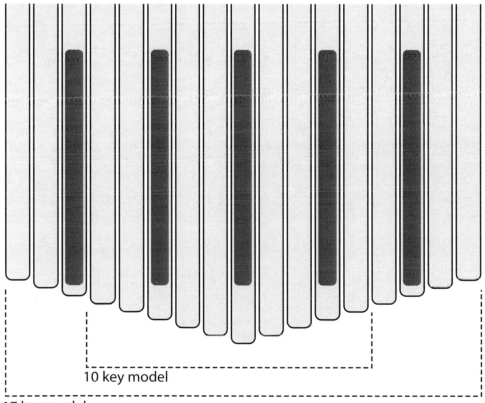

10 key model

17 key model

Kalimba tablature

To make playing the songs in this book as easy as possible, I've included an extra line of kalimba tablature right below the notation. This simple and intuitive system tells you exactly where to find the notes on your kalimba. It consists of two elements:

- **A number** telling you the key (tine) you're supposed to play
- **A vertical line** representing the middle of the instrument (the longest key, tuned to C) and indicating on which side of your kalimba to play.

Here's an example: **2|** means: play the **key 2** on the **left side** of your kalimba.

|3 means: play the **key 3** on the **right side** of your kalimba.

The lowest note of your instrument (the longest key, tuned to C) is represented by the number **1** (without any vertical line).

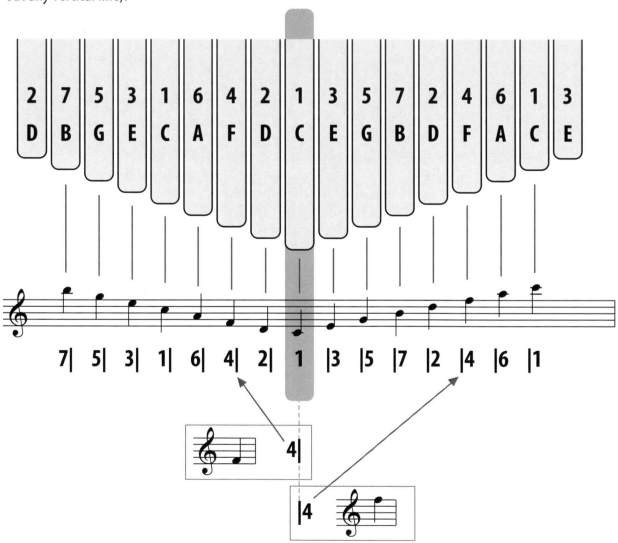

Tom Dooley

Hang down your head, Tom Doo - ley,_____
2| 2| 2| |3 |5 |7 |7_____

hang down your head and cry._____
2| 2| 2| |3 |5 |6|_____

Hang down your head, Tom Doo - ley,_____
2| 2| 2| |3 |5 |6| |6_____

poor boy, you're bound to die.
6| 6| |7 |5 |3 |5

2. This time tomorrow,
   reckon where I'll be?
   If it hadn't been for Grayson,
   I'd a-been in Tennessee.

3. This time tomorrow,
   reckon where I'll be?
   Down in some lonesome valley,
   hangin' from a white oak tree.

Cotton-eyed Joe

Where do you come from, where do you go?
|7 |7 |7 |6| |5 |7 |7 |7 |2|

Where do you come from, cot-ton-eyed Joe?
|7 |7 |7 |6| |5 |2| |3 |5 |5|

Come for to see you, come for to sing,
|7 |7 |7 |6| |5 |7 |7 |7 |2|

come for to show you my dia - mond ring.
|7 |7 |7 |6| 6| |5 |2| |3 |5 |5|

2. Do you remember a long time ago,
   there was a man called cotton-eyed Joe?
   Could have been married a long time ago,
   hadn't it been for cotton-eyed Joe.

3. Old bull fiddle and a shoe-string bow,
   wouldn't play nothin' like cotton-eyed Joe.
   Play it fast or play it slow,
   can't play nothin' like cotton-eyed Joe.

All the good times are past and gone

2. See that east-bound passenger train,
   coming around the bend.
   It's taking away my own true love,
   to never return again.

3. I wish dear Lord I'd never been born,
   or died when I was young.
   I never would've seen those two brown eyes,
   or heard your lying tongue.

4. See that lonesome turtle dove,
   flying from pine to pine.
   He's mourning for his own true love,
   just like I mourn for mine.

Amazing grace

1. A - maz - ing grace how sweet the
   2| |5 |7 |7 6| |5 |3

sounds, that saved a wretch like me. I
2| 2| |5 |7 |7 6| |2 |7

once was lost, but now am
|2 |7 |7 6| |5 |3

found; was blind but now I see.
2| 2| |5 |7 |7 6| |5

2. 'Twas grace that taught my heart to fear,
   And grace my fears relieved;
   How precious did that grace appear,
   The hour I first believed!

3. Through many dangers, toils and snares,
   I have already come;
   'Twas grace that brought me safe thus far,
   And grace will lead me home.

4. The Lord has promised good to me,
   His word my hope secures;
   He will my shield and portion be,
   As long as life endures.

5. Yes, when this flesh and heart shall fail,
   And mortal life shall cease;
   I shall possess, within the veil,
   A life of joy and peace.

6. The earth shall soon dissolve like snow,
   The sun forbear to shine;
   But God, who call'd me here below,
   Will be forever mine.

Buffalo gals

1. As I went walk-ing down the street, down the street,
|5 1 1 |3 |5 6| |5 |3 |5 4| 2|

down the street, a pret-ty girl I chanced to meet
6| |5 |3 |5 1 1 |3 |5 6| |5 |3

un-der the sil-ver-y moon.
|5 |5 |5 4| |3 2| 1

Chorus

Buf-fa-lo gals, will you
1| 1| |7 6| |5 |5

come out to-night, come out to-night, come out to-night,
6| |5 |5 |3 |5 4| 4| 2| 6| |5 |5 |3

Buf-fa-lo gals, will you come out to-night, and
1| 1| |7 6| |5 |5 6| |5 |5 |3 |3

dance by the light of the moon.
|5 |5 |5 4| |3 2| 1

2. I asked her would she have some talk,
have some talk, have some talk.
Her feet covered the whole sidewalk
as she stood close by me.

3. I asked her would she have a dance,
have a dance, have a dance.
I thought I might get a chance
to shake a foot with her.

4. I'd like to make that gal my wife,
gal my wife, gal my wife.
I'd be happy all my life.
If I had her by me.

Kum ba yah

2. Someone's crying, Lord, kum ba yah!

3. Someone's singing, Lord, kum ba yah!

4. Someone's praying, Lord, kum ba yah!

Over the river and through the woods—

O - ver the ri - ver and through the woods, to
|5 |5 |5 |5 |3 4| |5 |5 |5 |5

Grand - fath - er's house we go; The
1| 1| 1| |7 6| |5 |5

horse knows the way to car - ry the sleigh through the
4| 4| 4| 4| 4| |3 |3 |3 |3 |3 |3

white and drift - ed snow.___ Thanks - giv - ing day.
2| 2| 2| |3 2| |5 2| 2| 2| 1

2. Over the river and through the woods,
   to have a first-rate play;
   Oh, hear the bells ring, "Ting-a-ling-ling!"
   Hurrah for Thanksgiving Day!
   Over the river and through the woods,
   trot fast, my dapple gray!
   Spring over the ground, Like a hunting hound!
   For this is Thanksgiving Day.

3. Over the river and through the woods,
   and straight through the barnyard gate.
   We seem to go extremely slow
   it is so hard to wait!
   Over the river and through the woods,
   now Grandmother's cap I spy!
   Hurrah for the fun! Is the pudding done?
   Hurrah for the pumpkin pie!

Scarborough Fair

Are you go - ing to Scar - bor-ough Fair?
2| 2| 6| 6| 6| |3 4| |3 2|

Pars - ley, sage, rose - mar - y and thyme; Re -
6| 1| |2 1| 6| |7 |5 6| 6|

mem - ber me to one who lived there, ___ for
|2 |2 1| 6| 6| |5 4| |3 1 1

once she was a true love of mine.
2| 6| |5 4| |3 2| 1 2|

2. Tell her to make me a cambric shirt,
   parsley, sage, rosemary, and thyme;
   Without a seam or needlework,
   then she shall be a true love of mine.

3. Tell her to wash it in yonder well,
   parsley, sage, rosemary, and thyme;
   where never spring water or rain ever fell,
   and she shall be a true love of mine.

4. Tell her to dry it on yonder thorn,
   parsley, sage, rosemary, and thyme;
   Which never bore blossom since Adam was born,
   then she shall be a true love of mine.

5. Now he has asked me questions three,
   parsley, sage, rosemary, and thyme;
   I hope he'll answer as many for me
   before he shall be a true love of mine.

6. Tell him to buy me an acre of land,
   parsley, sage, rosemary, and thyme;
   Between the salt water and the sea sand,
   then he shall be a true love of mine.

7. Tell him to plough it with a ram's horn,
   parsley, sage, rosemary, and thyme;
   And sow it all over with one pepper corn,
   and he shall be a true love of mine.

8. Tell him to sheer't with a sickle of leather,
   parsley, sage, rosemary, and thyme;
   And bind it up with a peacock feather.
   And he shall be a true love of mine.

9. Tell him to thrash it on yonder wall,
   parsley, sage, rosemary, and thyme,
   and never let one corn of it fall,
   then he shall be a true love of mine.

10. When he has done and finished his work.
    Parsley, sage, rosemary, and thyme:
    Oh, tell him to come and he'll have his shirt,
    and he shall be a true love of mine.

Good night, ladies

Good night, la - dies!   Good night, la - dies!
|7 |5 2| |5 |7 |5 6| 6|

Good night, la - dies, we're go-ing to leave you now.
|7 |5 1| 1| 1| |7 |7 |7 6| 6| |5

Mer - ri - ly we roll a - long, roll a - long, roll a - long,
|7 6| |5 6| |7 |7 |7   6| 6| 6| |7 |2 |2

mer - ri - ly we roll a - long, o'er the dark blue sea.
|7 6| |5 6| |7 |7 |7   6| 6| |7 6| |5

2. Farewell, ladies! (3x)
   We're going to leave you now.
   Merrily we roll along,
   roll along, roll along,
   merrily we roll along,
   o'er the deep blue sea.

3. Sweet dreams, ladies! (3x)
   We're going to leave you now.
   Merrily we roll along,
   roll along, roll along,
   merrily we roll along,
   o'er the deep blue sea.

Oh! Susanna

I came from A - la - ba - ma with my
1 2| |3 |5 |5 6| |5 |3 1 1 2|

ban - jo on my knee, I'm goin' to Lou' - si -
|3 |3 2| 1 2| 1 2| |3 |5 |5 6|

a - na, my Su - san - na for to see. Oh! Su -
|5 |3 1 2| |3 |3 2| 2| 1 4| 4|

san - na, oh don't you cry for me, for I come from A - la -
6| 6| 6| |5 |5 |3 1 2| 1 2| |3 |5 |5 6|

ba - ma with my ban - jo on my knee.
|5 |3 1 1 2| |3 |3 2| 2| 1

2. I had a dream the other night
   when ev'rything was still;
   I thought I saw Susanna
   a-comin' down the hill;
   the buckwheat cake was in her mouth,
   the tear was in her eye;
   says I, I'm comin' from the south,
   Susanna, don't you cry.
   Oh! Susanna ...

3. I soon will be in New Orleans,
   and then I'll look around,
   and when I find Susanna
   I'll fall upon the ground.
   And if I do not find her,
   then I will surely die,
   and when I'm dead and buried,
   Susanna, don't you cry.
   Oh! Susanna ...

Banks of Sacramento

A bull - y ship and a bull - y - crew,
|3 |5 |5 |3 |5 |5 6| |5 |3

doo - da! Doo - da! A bull - y mate and a
|3 2| |3 2| |3 |5 |5 |3 |5 |5

cap - tain, too, doo - da! Doo - da - day! Then
6| |5 |3 2| 4| |3 2| 1 |3

blow, ye winds, hi - oh, for Cal - i - forn - i -
1 1 |3 |5 1| 1| 6| 6| 1| 6|

o, there's plent - y of gold, so I've been told, on the
|5 |5 |5 |5 |5 |3 |5 6| |5 |3 |3 |3

banks of Sac - ra - men - to!
2| 4| |3 |3 2| 1

2. Oh, heave, my lads, oh heave and sing,
   oh, heave and make those oak sticks sing.

3. Our money gone, we shipped to go,
   around Cape Horn, through ice and snow.

4. Oh, around the Horn with a mainskys'l set
   around Cape Horn and we're all wringin' wet.

5. Around Cape Horn in the month of May,
   with storm winds blowing every day.

Mary had a little lamb

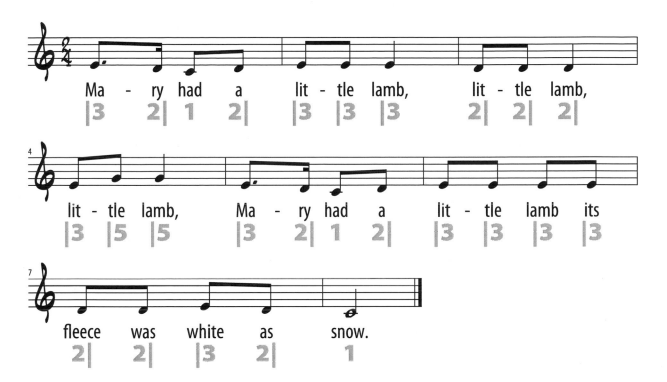

Ma - ry had a lit - tle lamb, lit - tle lamb,
|3 2| 1 2| |3 |3 |3 2| 2| 2|

lit - tle lamb, Ma - ry had a lit - tle lamb its
|3 |5 |5 |3 2| 1 2| |3 |3 |3 |3

fleece was white as snow.
2| 2| |3 2| 1

2. And everywhere that Mary went,
   Mary went, Mary went,
   everywhere that Mary went
   the lamb was sure to go.

3. It followed her to school one day,
   school one day, school one day,
   it followed her to school one day
   which was against the rule.

4. It made the children laugh and play,
   laugh and play, laugh and play,
   it made the children laugh and play
   to see a lamb at school.

5. And so the teacher turned it out,
   turned it out, turned it out,
   and so the teacher turned it out
   but still it lingered near.

6. And waited patiently about,
   patiently, patiently,
   and waited patiently about
   till Mary did appear.

7. "Why does the lamb love Mary so,
   Mary so, Mary so?"
   "Why does the lamb love Mary so?"
   the eager children cry.

8. "Because the lamb loves Mary so,
   Mary so, Mary so",
   "Because the lamb loves Mary so",
   the teacher did reply.

Way down the old plank road

I'd rath-er be in Rich-mond with
2| 2| 2| 2| |3 |5 |5 |5

all the hail and rain, than to be in
|7 6| |5 |3 |5 2| 2| 2| |3

Geor-gia, boys, tied to a ball and chain. Won't___
|5 |5 |5 |5 |5 |5 |5 |3 2| |7____

__ get drunk no more, boys, won't_____ get drunk no
____ 6| |5 |3 |5 |5 |7_____ 6| |5 |3

more. Won't_____ get drunk no more, boys,
2| |7____ 6| |5 |3 |5 |5

way down the old plank road.
6| 6| 6| |7 6| |5

2. I went down to Mobile, but I got on the gravel train,
   very next thing they heard of me, had on that ball and chain.
   Won't get drunk no more, boys ...

3. Doney, oh dear Doney, what makes you treat me so,
   caused me to wear that ball and chain, now my ankle's sore
   Won't get drunk no more, boys ...

4. Knoxville is a pretty place, Memphis is a beauty,
   wanta see them pretty girls, hop to Chattanoogie.
   Won't get drunk no more, boys ...

5. I'm going to build me a scaffold on some mountain high,
   so I can see my Doney girl as she goes riding by.
   Won't get drunk no more, boys ...

6. My wife died on Friday night, Saturday she was buried,
   Sunday was my courtin' day, Monday I got married.
   Won't get drunk no more, boys ...

7. Eighteen pounds of meat a week, whiskey here to sell,
   how can a young man stay at home, pretty girls look so well.
   Won't get drunk no more, boys ...

Will the circle be unbroken

Will   the   cir - cle_____   be   un - bro - ken,_____
2| |5 |5 |5_____ |7   6| |5 |7

_____   by   and   by,   Lord,   by   and   by.
_____ |7   6| |5   6| |5 |3   2|

There's   a   bet - ter_____   home   a - wait - ing_____
2| |5 |5 |5_____ |7 |2 |2 |7

_____   in   the   sky,   Lord,   in   the   sky.
_____ |7 |5 |7 |7 |7   6| |5

2. I said to the undertaker,
   "Undertaker please drive slow.
   For that body you are carrying,
   Lord, I hate to see her go."

3. Well I followed close behind her,
   tried to hold up and be brave.
   But I could not hide my sorrow,
   when they laid her in that grave.

4. I went back home, Lord, that home was lonesome.
   Since my mother, she was gone,
   all my brothers and sisters crying.
   What a home so sad and alone.

Michael, row the boat ashore

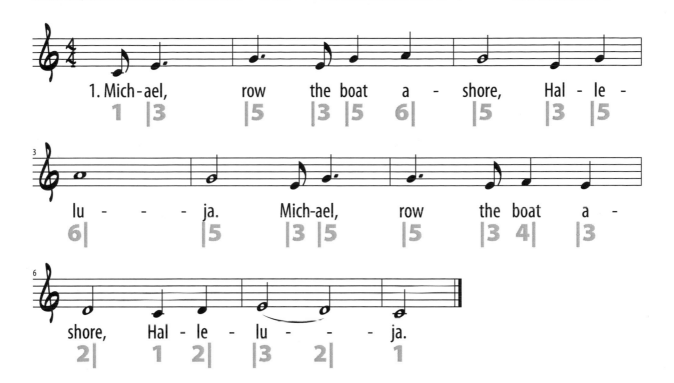

1. Mich-ael, row the boat a - shore, Hal - le - lu - - - ja. Mich-ael, row the boat a - shore, Hal - le - lu - - - ja.

2. Michael boat a gospelboat, Halleluja ...

3. Brother lend a helping hand, Halleluja ...

4. Sister help to trim the sail, Halleluja ...

5. Boasting talk will sink your soul, Halleluja ...

6. Jordan-stream is deep and wide, Halleluja ...

7. Jesus stand on the other side, Halleluja ...

Shenandoah

Oh   Shen - an - doah,_____   I   long   to
1   1   1   1_____   2| |3 |5

hear   you._____   A - way_____   you   rol - ling
|5 |3_____   1| |7   6|_____ |5   6| |5

riv - er,_____   oh   Shen - an - doah,_____   I   long   to
|3 |5_____ |5   6| 6| 6|_____ |3 |5 |3

see   you._____   A - way,_____   I'm   bound   a -
2| 1_____   2| |3   1 |3   6|

way_____   a - cross   the   wide_____   Mis - sour - i._____
|5_____   1 |3 |3 |3   2| 2| 1

2. Oh Shenandoah,
   I love your daughter,
   away, you rolling river.
   For her I'd cross,
   your roaming waters,
   away, I'm bound away,
   'cross the wide Missouri.

3. 'Tis seven years,
   since last I've seen you,
   away, you rolling river.
   'Tis seven years,
   since last I've seen you,
   away, we're bound away,
   'cross the wide Missouri.

House of the Rising Sun

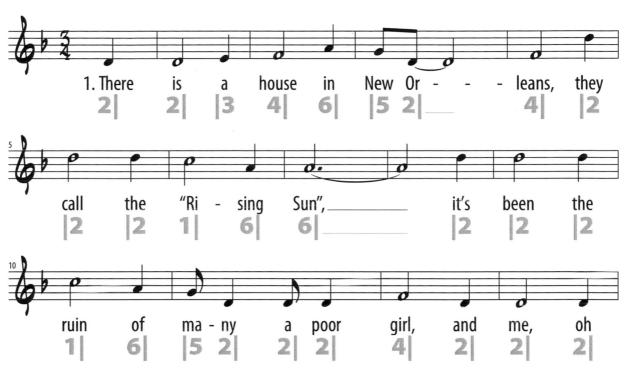

1. There is a house in New Or - - - leans, they
   2| 2| |3 4| 6| |5 2|_____ 4| |2

call the "Ri - sing Sun",_____ it's been the
|2 |2 1| 6| 6|_____ |2 |2 |2

ruin of ma - ny a poor girl, and me, oh
1| 6| |5 2| 2| 2| 4| 2| 2| 2|

Lord, I'm one._____
|5 4| 2|_____

2. If I had listened what Mamma said,
   I'd been at home today.
   Being so young and foolish, poor boy,
   let a rambler lead me astray.

3. Go tell my baby sister,
   never do like I have done,
   to shun that house in New Orleans,
   they call the Rising Sun.

4. My mother she's a tailor;
   She sold those new blue jeans.
   My sweetheart, he's a drunkard, Lord,
   drinks down in New Orleans.

5. The only thing a drunkard needs,
   is a suitcase and a trunk.
   The only time he's satisfied,
   is when he's on a drunk.

6. Fills his glasses to the brim,
   passes them around.
   Only pleasure he gets out of life,
   is hoboin' from town to town.

7. One foot is on the platform,
   and the other one on the train.
   I'm going back to New Orleans,
   to wear that ball and chain.

8. Going back to New Orleans,
   my race is almost run.
   Going back to spend the rest of my life,
   beneath that Rising Sun.

Home! Sweet home!

'Mid   plea - sures and pal - a - ces
1 2| |3   4| 6| |5 |3 |5

though   we may roam. Be it ev - er so
4| |3 4| 2| |3   1 2| |3   4| 6|

hum - ble, there's no   place like home.   A
|5 |3 |5   4| |3 4| 2| 1 |5

charm from the skies seems to hal - low us
1| |7 6| |5 |3 |5   4| |3 4| 2|

there, which seek thro' the world, is ne'er
|3 |5   1| |7 6| |5 |3 |5

met   with else - where. Home!   Home!
4| |3 4| 2| 1 |5   4| 2|

Sweet, sweet   home! There's no   place like
1   2| |3 |5   1| |7 6| |5

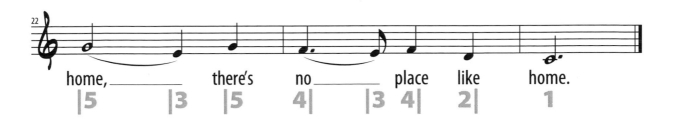

|5 |3 |5   4| |3 4| 2| 1

home,_____ there's no_____ place like   home.

2. An exile from home, spendor dazzles in vain,
   oh, give me my lowly thatched cottage again;
   The birds singing gaily, that come at my call;
   Give me them, with that peace of mind, dearer than all.

3. To thee, I'll return, overburdened with care,
   the heart's dearest solace will smile on me there.
   No more from that cottage again will I roam,
   be it ever so humble, there's no place like home.

Beautiful brown eyes

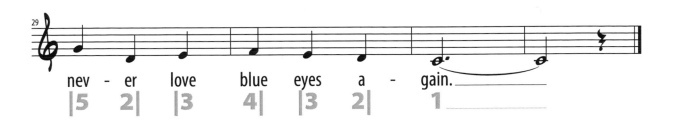

nev - er love blue eyes a - gain.

|5 2| |3 4| |3 2| 1

2. I staggered into the barroom,
   I fell down on the floor.
   And the very last words that I uttered,
   "I'll never get drunk any more."
   Beautiful, beautiful brown eyes ...

3. Seven long years I've been married,
   I wish I was single again.
   A woman don't know half her troubles,
   until she has married a man.
   Beautiful, beautiful brown eyes ...

Camptown races

The Camp - town la - dies sing this song,
|5 |5 |5 |3 |5 6| |5 |3

doo - dah, doo - dah! The Camp - town race - track's
|3 2| |3 2| |5 |5 |5 |3 |5

five miles long, oh, doo - dah day! I
6| |5 |3 2| |3 2| 1 |5

went down there with my hat caved in, doo - dah,
|5 |5 |3 |5 |5 6| |5 |3 |3 2|

doo - dah! I go back home with a
|3 2| |5 |5 |5 |3 |5 |5

pock - et full of tin, oh, doo - dah - day!
6| 6| |5 |5 |3 2| |3 2| 1

Goin' to run all night! Goin' to run all day! I'll
1 1 |3 |5 1| 6| 6| 1| 6| |5 |3

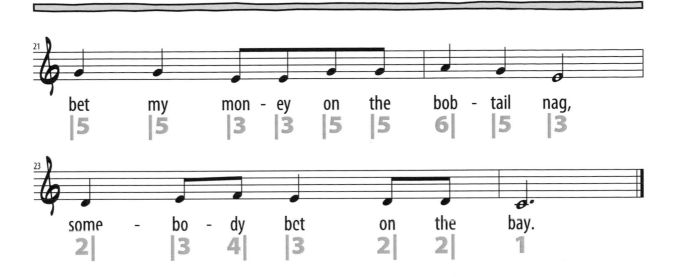

bet my mon-ey on the bob-tail nag,
|5 |5 |3 |3 |5 |5 6| |5 |3

some-bo-dy bet on the bay.
2| |3 4| |3 2| 2| 1

2. De long tail filly and de big black hoss, doo-dah, doo-dah!
   Dey fly de track and dey both cut across, oh, doo-dah-day!
   De blind hoss sticken in a big mud hole, doo-dah, doo-dah!
   Can't touch bottom wid a ten foot pole, oh, doo-dah-day!

Chorus

3. Old muley cow come on to de track, doo-dah, doo-dah!
   De bob-tail fling her ober his back, oh, doo-dah-day!
   Den fly along like a rail-road car, doo-dah, doo-dah!
   Runnin' a race wid a shootin' star, oh, doo-dah-day!

Chorus

4. See dem flyin' on a ten mile heat, doo-dah, doo-dah!
   Round de race track, den repeat, oh, doo-dah-day!
   I win my money on de bob-tail nag, doo-dah, doo-dah!
   I keep my money in an old tow-bag, oh, doo-dah-day!

The last rose of summer

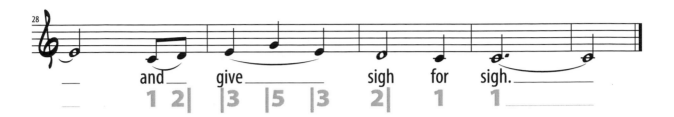

and__ give_____ sigh for sigh._____

1 2| |3 |5 |3 2| 1 1

2. I'll not leave thee, thou lone one!
   To pine on the stem;
   Since the lovely are sleeping,
   go, sleep thou with them.
   Thus kindly I scatter,
   thy leaves o'er the bed,
   where thy mates of the garden
   lie scentless and dead.

3. So soon may I follow,
   when friendships decay,
   and from Love's shining circle
   the gems drop away.
   When true hearts lie withered,
   and fond ones are flown.
   Oh! who would inhabit
   this bleak world alone?

Old folks at home

Way down up - on the Swan - ee Ri - ver,
|3 2| 1 |3 2| 1 1| 6| 1|

far, far a - way, that's where my heart is
|5 |3 1 2| |3 2| 1 |3 2|

tur - ning ev - er, that's where the old folks stay.
1 1| 6| 1| |5 |3 1 2| 2| 1

All up and down the whole cre - a - tion, sad - ly I
|3 2| 1 |3 2| 1 1| 6| 1| |5 |3 1

roam; still long - ing for the old plan - ta - tion
2| |3 2| 1 |3 2| 1 1| 6| 1|

Chorus

and for the old folks at home. All the world is
|5 |3 1 2| 2| 2| 1 |7 1| 2| |5

sad and drear - y ev - 'ry - where I
|5 6| |5 1| 1| 6| 4| 6|

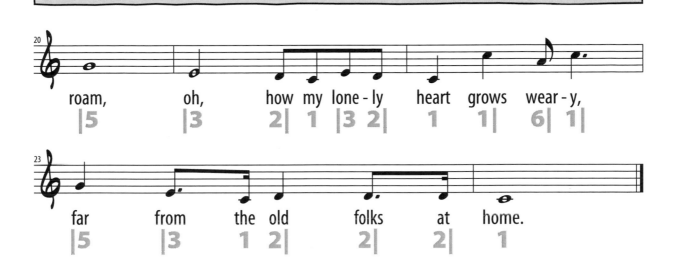

2. All 'round the little farm I wandered,
   when I was young.
   Then many happy days I squandered,
   many the songs I sung,
   when I was playing with my brother,
   happy was I.
   Oh, take me to my kind old mother,
   there let me live and die.

3. One little hut among the bushes,
   one that I love,
   still sadly to my mem'ry rushes,
   no matter where I rove,
   when shall I see the bees a-humming,
   all 'round the comb,
   when shall I hear the banjo strumming,
   down by my good old home.

What shall we do with the drunken sailor

What shall we do with the drun - ken sai - lor,
6| 6| 6| 6| 6| 6| 6| 2| 4| 6|

what shall we do with the drun - ken sai - lor,
|5 |5 |5 |5 |5 |5 |5 1 |3 |5

what shall we do with the drun - ken sai - lor
6| 6| 6| 6| 6| 6| 6| |7 1| |2

ear - ly in the mor - ning. Hoo - ray and up she ri - ses,
1| 6| |5 |3 2| 2| 6| 6| 6| 6| 2| 4| 6|

hoo - ray and up she ri - ses, hoo - ray and
|5 |5 |5 |5 1 |3 |5 6| 6| 6|

up she ri - ses ear - ly in the mor - ning.
6| |7 1| |2 1| 6| |5 |3 2| 2|

2. Give him a dose of salent water, early ...

3. Give him a dash with a besoms rubber, early ...

4. Pull out the plug and wet him all over, early ...

5. Heave him by the leg in a running bowlin', early ...

6. That's what to do with a drunken sailor, early ...

Brahms' Lullaby

2. Lullaby, and good night,
your mother's delight,
shining angels beside my darling abide.
Soft and warm is your bed,
close your eyes and rest your head.
Soft and warm is your bed,
close your eyes and rest your head.

3. Sleepyhead, close your eyes,
mother's right here beside you.
I'll protect you from harm,
you will wake in my arms.
Guardian angels are near,
so sleep on, with no fear.
Guardian angels are near,
so sleep on, with no fear.

Finnegan's wake

Tim Fin - ne - gan lived in Walk - in' Street, a
|5 |3 |3 |3 |3 2| |3 6| 6| |7

gen - tle I - rish - man might - y odd. He had a brogue both
1| |7 6| 6| |5 |3 2| 2| |5 |3 |3 |3 2|

rich and sweet, and to rise in the world he
|3 6| 6| 6| |7 |1 |7 |7 6| |5

car - ried a hod. Now Tim had a sort o' the tip - plin way, with a
6| 6| |7 1| 1| 1| 1| 1| 1| |2 2| 1| |7 6| |5 5|

love for the liq - our poor Tim was born. To help him on his
1| 1| 1| 1| 1| |2 1| |7 6| |5 1| 1| 1| |2

way each day, he'd a drop of the cray - thur ev - 'ry morn.
1| |7 6| |5 5| 6| 6| 6| 6| |5 6| 7| 1|

Whack for the hur - rah, dance to your part - ner round the floor ye
|3 |3 |3 |3 2| |3 6| 6| 6| |7 1| |7 6| |7

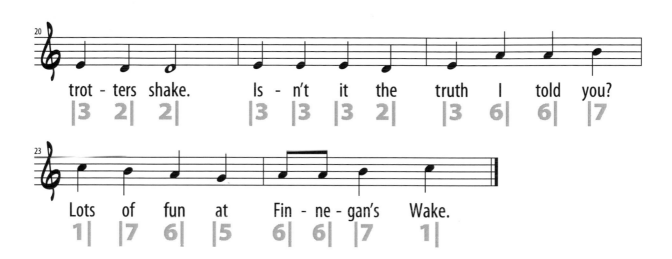

trot - ters shake. |3 2| 2| Is - n't it the truth I told you? |3 |3 |3 2| |3 6| 6| |7

Lots of fun at Fin - ne - gan's Wake. 1| |7 6| |5 6| 6| |7 1|

2. One morning Tim was rather full,
   his head felt heavy which made him shake.
   He fell from a ladder and he broke his skull,
   so they carried him home his corpse to wake.
   They rolled him up in a nice clean sheet,
   and laid him out upon the bed.
   A bottle of whiskey at his feet,
   and a barrel of porter at his head.
   Whack for the hurrah ...

3. His friends assembled at the wake,
   and Missus Finnegan called for lunch.
   First she brought out tay and cake,
   then pipes, tobacco and whiskey punch.
   Then Biddy O'Brien began to cry,
   "Such a nice clean corpse, did you ever see,
   Tim, mavourneen! Why did you die?".
   "Will ye hould your gob?" said Paddy McGee.
   Whack for the hurrah ...

4. Then Maggie O'Connor took up the cry,
   "O Biddy" says she "you're wrong, I'm sure".
   Biddy, she gave her a belt in the gob,
   and sent her sprawling on the floor.
   And then the war did soon engage,
   t'was woman to woman and man to man.
   Shillelaigh law was all the rage,
   and a row and a ruction soon began.
   Whack for the hurrah ...

5. Mickey Maloney ducked his head,
   when a bucket of whiskey flew at him.
   It missed, and falling on the bed,
   the liquor scattered over Tim.
   Now the spirits new life gave the corpse, my joy!
   Bedad he revives, see how he rises!
   Cryin while he ran around like blazes,
   „Thunderin' blazes, do ye think I'm dead?"

Aura Lee

Please note: Due to the note f in bar 13 you can play this song only on a 17 key instrument.

2. In thy blush the rose was born,
   music, when you spake,
   through thine azure eye the morn,
   sparkling seemed to break.
   Aura Lee, Aura Lee,
   birds of crimson wing,
   never song have sung to me,
   as in that sweet spring.
   Aura Lee! Aura Lee! ...

3. Aura Lee, the bird may flee,
   the willow's golden hair,
   swing through winter fitfully,
   on the stormy air.
   Yet if thy blue eyes I see,
   gloom will soon depart;
   for to me, sweet Aura Lee
   is sunshine through the heart.
   Aura Lee! Aura Lee! ...

4. When the mistletoe was green,
   midst the winter's snows,
   sunshine in thy face was seen,
   kissing lips of rose.
   Aura Lee, Aura Lee,
   Take my golden ring;
   Love and light return with thee,
   and swallows with the spring.
   Aura Lee! Aura Lee! ...

Morning has broken

London Bridge is falling down

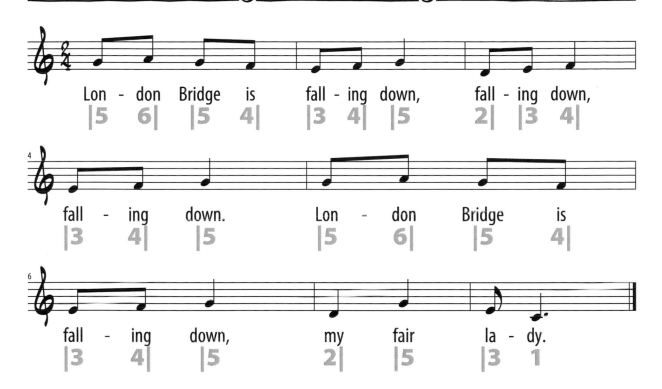

Lon - don Bridge is fall - ing down,
|5 6| |5 4| |3 4| |5

fall - ing down,
2| |3 4|

fall - ing down.
|3 4| |5

Lon - don Bridge is
|5 6| |5 4|

fall - ing down,
|3 4| |5

my fair
2| |5

la - dy.
|3 1

2. Take a key and lock her up,
lock her up, lock her up.
Take a key and lock her up,
my fair lady.

3. How will we build it up,
build it up, build it up?
How will we build it up,
my fair lady.

4. Build it up with gold and silver,
gold and silver, gold and silver.
Build it up with gold and silver,
my fair lady.

5. Gold and silver I have none,
I have none, I have none.
Gold and silver I have none,
my fair lady.

6. Build it up with needles and pins,
needles and pins, needles and pins.
Build it up with needles and pins,
my fair lady.

7. Pins and needles bend and break,
bend and break, bend and break.
Pins and needles bend and break,
my fair lady.

8. Build it up with wood and clay,
wood and clay, wood and clay.
Build it up with wood and clay,
my fair lady.

9. Wood and clay will wash away,
wash away, wash away.
Wood and clay will wash away,
my fair lady.

10. Build it up with stone so strong,
stone so strong, stone so strong.
Build it up with stone so strong,
my fair lady.

11. Stone so strong will last so long,
last so long, last so long.
Stone so strong will last so long,
my fair lady.

Long journey home

Lost all my mon-ey but a two dol-lar bill,
2| 2| |3 |5 |5 |5 |5 |7 |7 6| |5

two dol - lar bill boys, two dol - lar bill.
|7 |7 6| |5 |5 |3 |5 |3 2|

Lost all my mon-ey but a two dol - lar
2| 2| |3 |5 |5 |5 |5 |7 |7 6|

bill, I'm on my long journ-ey home._____
|5 |2 |2 |7 6| |7 6| |5_____

2. Cloudy in the west and it looks like rain,
   looks like rain boy, looks like rain.
   Cloudy in the west and it looks like rain,
   I'm on my long journey home.

3. Black smoke a-rising and it surely is a train,
   surely is a train boys, surely is a train.
   Black smoke a-rising and it surely is a train,
   I'm on my long journey home.

4. Homesick and lonesome and I'm feeling kind of blue,
   feeling kind of blue boys, feeling kind of blue.
   Homesick and lonesome and I'm feeling kind of blue,
   I'm on my long journey home.

5. It's starting raining and I've got to go home,
   I've got to go home boys, I've got to go home.
   It's starting raining and I've got to go home,
   I'm on my long journey home.

Twinkle, twinkle, little star

2. When the blazing sun is gone,
   when he nothing shines upon,
   then you show your little light,
   twinkle, twinkle, all the night.

3. Then the traveller in the dark,
   thanks you for your tiny spark,
   he could not see which way to go,
   if you did not twinkle so.

4. In the dark blue sky you keep,
   and often through my curtains peep,
   for you never shut your eye,
   till the sun is in the sky.

5. As your bright and tiny spark,
   lights the traveller in the dark,
   though I know not what you are,
   twinkle, twinkle, little star.

Old Mac Donald had a farm

Old   Mac   Do - nald   had   a   farm,   E   I   E   I
|5 |5   2| 2| |3 |3   2| |7 |7   6| 6|

O!   And   on   his   farm   he   had   some   chicks,
|5   2| |5 |5 |5   2| |3 |3   2|

E   I   E   I   O!   With   a   chick - chick   here   and   a
|7 |7   6| 6| |5   2| 2| |5 |5 |5   2| 2|

chick - chick   there.   Here   a   chick,   there   a   chick,
|5 |5 |5 |5 |5 |5 |5 |5 |5

ev - ry - where   a   chick - chick.   Old   Mac   Do - nald
|5 |5 |5 |5 |5 |5 |5 |5   2| 2|

had   a   farm,   E   I   E   I   O!
|3 |3   2| |7 |7   6| 6| |5

2. ... he had some geese ...
   With a gabble-gabble here ...

3. ... he had a pig ...
   With an oinck-oink here ...

4. ... he had some ducks ...
   With a quack-quack here ...

5. ... he had a cow ...
   With a moo-moo here ...

Roll in my sweet baby's arms

2. Now where was you last Friday night while I was lyin' in jail.
   Walkin' the streets with another man you wouldn't even go my bail,
   then I'll roll in my sweet baby's arms.

3. I know your parents don't like me they drove me away from your door.
   And my life's too bluer never to wearing more,
   then I'll roll in my sweet baby's arms.

My home's across the smoky mountains

My home's a - cross the smo - ky moun - tains. My
|7 |7 |2 |7 6| |5 |3 |5 2| |7

home's a - cross the smo - ky moun - - tains. My
6| 6| 6| 6| |5 6| |7 |2 |7 |5

home's a - cross the smo - ky moun - tains and I'll
|7 |2 |7 6| |5 |3 |5 2| |5 |5

ne - ver get to see you a - ny more, more,
6| |5 6| |5 |7 6| |5 |3 |5 |5

more, I'll ne - ver get to see you a - ny more.
2| 5| 6| 6| 6| 6| |7 6| |5 |3 |5

2. Goodbye honey, sugar darling.
   Goodbye honey, sugar darling.
   Goodbye honey, sugar darling,
   and I'll never get to see you any more, more, more,
   I'll never get to see you any more.

3. Rock my baby, feed her candy.
   Rock my baby, feed her candy.
   Rock my baby, feed her candy,
   and I'll never get to see you any more, more, more,
   I'll never get to see you any more.

Colorado trail

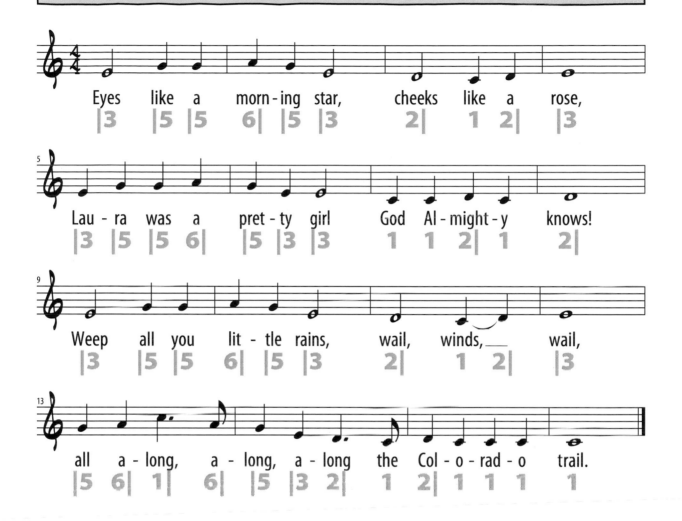

Eyes like a morn-ing star, cheeks like a rose,
|3 |5 |5 6| |5 |3 2| 1 2| |3

Lau - ra was a pret - ty girl God Al - might - y knows!
|3 |5 |5 6| |5 |3 |3 1 1 2| 1 2|

Weep all you lit - tle rains, wail, winds,___ wail,
|3 |5 |5 6| |5 |3 2| 1 2| |3

all a - long, a - long, a - long the Col - o - rad - o trail.
|5 6| 1| 6| |5 |3 2| 1 2| 1 1 1 1

On top of Old Smokey

On top of old Smo - - - key,
1 1 |3 |5 1| 6|

all cov – ered with snow;____
4| 4| |5 6| |5____

I lost my true lov - - er
1 1 |3 |5 |5 2|

a – court – ing too slow.____
|3 4| |3 2| 1____

Up on the housetop

Up   on   the   house - top_____   rein - deer   pause,
|5 |5   6| |5 |3   2| 1 |3 |5

out   jumps   good   old   San - ta   Claus.   Down   through the   chim - ney   with
6| 6| |5 |3   2| |5 |5 |5 |5   6| |5 |3   2|

lots   of   toys,   all   for   the   lit - tle   ones'
1 |3 |5   6| 6| 6| |5 |5 |3

Christ - mas   joys.   Ho,   ho,   ho!   Who   would - n't   go!
2| |5   1   4| 4| 6| |5 |5 |5 |3

Ho,   ho,   ho!   Who   would - n't   go!   Up   on   the   house - top,
2| 4| 4| |3 |5   5| 1 |5 |5   6| |5 |3

click, click, click.   Down   through   the   chim - ney   with   good   Saint   Nick.
4| |5   6| |5 |5   6| |5 |3 |3   2| |5   1

When the saints go marchin' in

Oh, when the saints go mar-chin' in, oh, when the
1 |3 4| |5 1 |3 4| |5 1 |3 4|

saints go mar-chin' in, I want to be a-mong the
|5 |3 1 |3 2| |3 |3 2| 1 1 |3 |5

num-ber, oh, when the saints go mar-chin' in.
|5 4| 4| |3 4| |5 |3 1 2| 1

2. And when the stars begin to shine ...

3. When Gabriel blows in his horn ...

4. And when the sun refuse to shine ...

5. And when they gather round the throne ...

6. And when they crown him King of Kings ...

7. And on that halleluja-day ...

Pop! Goes the weasel

All a - round the cob - bler's bench, the
1 1 2| 2| |3 |5 |3 1 2|

mon - key chased the wea - - sel. The
1 1 2| 2| |3 1 2|

mon - key thought 'twas all in good fun,
1 1 2| 2| |3 |5 |3 1

Pop! Goes the wea - - - sel.
6| 2| 4| 2| 1

2. A penny for a spool of thread,
a penny for a needle.
That's the way the money goes,
Pop! Goes the weasel.

3. Jimmy's got the whooping cough
and Timmy's got the measles.
That's the way the story goes
Pop! Goes the weasel.

Row, row, row your boat

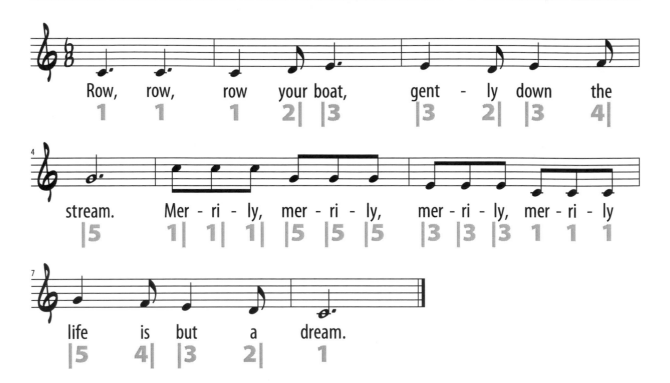

Cumberland Gap

Cum - ber - land   Gap's   a   fine   old   place,
1   1   2| 4| 4| 6| 1| |2

three   kinds   of   wa - ter   to   wash   your   face.
|2   1| 1| 6| |5   4| |5   4| 4|

Lay   down   boys,   take   a   lit – tle   nap,
1   2| 4| 6| 6| 1| 1| |2

four - teen   miles___   to   Cum - ber - land   Gap.
|2   1| 6| |5   4| |5   4| 4| 4|

2. Me and my wife and my wife's pap,
   we all live down in Cumberland Gap.
   Me and my wife and my wife's pap,
   we all live down in Cumberland Gap.

3. Cumberland Gap with its cliffs and rocks,
   home of the panther, bear and fox.
   Cumberland Gap with its cliffs and rocks,
   home of the panther, bear and fox.

Down by the riverside

1. I'm goin' to lay down my hea - vy load, ___
|7 |7 6| |7 2| |3 |5 |5 6|

Down by the ri - ver - side,
|7 |7 6| |7 6| |5

Down by the
6| 6| |5

ri - ver - side,
6| |5 6|

Down by the ri - ver - side, I'm goin' to
|7 |7 6| |7 6| |5 |7 |7 6|

lay down my hea - vy load, ___
|7 2| |3 |5 |5 6|

Down by the
|7 |7 6|

ri - ver - side, I ain't a - gon - na stu - dy war no more.
|7 6| |5 |5 6| 6| 6| 6| 6| |1 |7 6| |5

I ain't a - gon - na stu - dy war no
5| 6| 6| |7 |7 1| 1| 1| 1|

more, I ain't a - gon - na stu - dy war no
1| 1| |5 |5 6| 6| |7 |7 |7 |7

more, I ain't a-gon-na stu-dy war no more.
|7 |7 6| 6| |7 |7 6| 6| |5 6| |7

stu-dy____ war no____ more.
6| |2 1| |7 |7 6| |5

2. I'm goin' to lay down my sword and shield ...

3. I'm goin' to put on my travelin' shoes ...

4. I'm goin' to put on my starry crown ...

5. Gonna put on my golden shoes ...

6. Gonna talk with the Prince of Peace ...

7. Gonna shake hands around the world ...

Jolly good fellow

For he's a jol - ly good fel - - -
1 |3 |3 |3 2| |3 4|

low, for he's a jol - ly good fel - -
|3 |3 2| 2| 2| 1 2| |3

low, for he's a jol - ly good fel - -
1 1 |3 |3 |3 2| |3 4|

low, which no - bo - dy can de - ny! _____
6| 6| |5 |5 |5 4| 2| 1 _____

2. We won't go home until morning, (3x)
   'till daylight doth appear.
   'Till daylight doth appear,
   'till daylight doth appear.
   We won't go home until morning, (3x)
   'till daylight doth appear.

Foggy mountain top

2. If I'd only listened to what my mama said,
   I would not be here today.
   Lying around this old jailhouse,
   wasting my poor life away.
   If I was on some foggy mountain top ...

3. Oh she caused me to weep, she caused me to mourn,
   she caused me to leave my home.
   Oh the lonesome pines and the good old times,
   I'm on my way back home.
   If I was on some foggy mountain top ...

Give me that old time religion

Give me that old time re - li - gion,
1 1 2| 4| 4| 4| 2| 1 4| 4| 4|

give me that old time re - li - gion, give me that old time re - li - gion,____ it's
|5 |5 6| |5 4| 4| 4| |5 6| 6| 6| |5 4|____ 2|

good e - nough____ for me. Just give me that me. 1. It was
1 4| 4|____ |5 4| 1 1 1 2| 4| 1 2|

good for the He - brew chil - dren, it was good for the He - brew
4| 4| 4| 4| 4| 2| 1 |3 4| |5 |5 |5 |5 6|

child - ren, it was good for the He - brew child - ren, and it's
|5 4| 4| |5 6| 6| 6| 6| 6| |5 4| 2| 2|

good e - nough____ for me. 2. It will me.
1 4| 4|____ |5 4| 1 2| 4|

2. It will do when the world's on fire,
   it will do when the world's on fire,
   it will do when the world's on fire,
   and it's good enough for me.

Goin' across the mountain

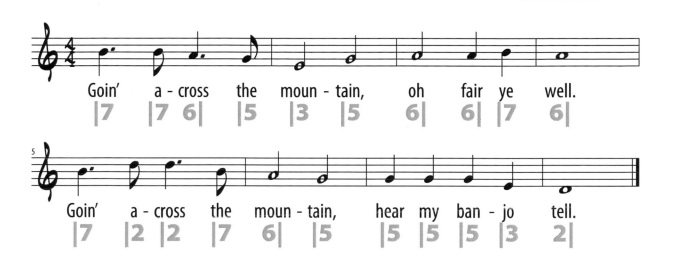

Goin' a-cross the moun-tain, oh fair ye well.
|7 |7 6| |5 |3 |5 |6| |6| |7 |6|

Goin' a-cross the moun-tain, hear my ban-jo tell.
|7 |2 |2 |7 |6| |5 |5| |5| |5| |3 |2|

2. Going across the mountain,
   join the boys in blue.
   When this war is over,
   I'll come back to you.

3. Got my rations on my back,
   my powder it is dry.
   Going across the mountain,
   Crissie don't you cry.

4. Waitin' 'fore it's good daylight,
   if nothing happens to me,
   I'll be way down yonder
   in old Tennessee.

5. 'Spect you'll miss me when I'm gone,
   but I'm going through,
   When this fightin's over,
   I'll come back to you.

Poor Paddy works on the railway

2. In eighteen hundred and forty-two
   I didn't know what I should do.
   I didn't know what I should do,
   to work upon the railway, the railway,
   I'm weary of the railway,
   poor Paddy works on the railway.

3. In eighteen hundred and forty-three
   I sailed away across the sea.
   I sailed away across the sea,
   to work upon the railway, the railway,
   I'm weary of the railway,
   poor Paddy works on the railway

4. In eighteen hundred and forty-four
   I landed on Columbia's shore.
   I landed on Columbia's shore,
   to work upon the railway, the railway.
   I'm weary of the railway,
   poor Paddy works on the railway.

5. In eighteen hundred and forty-five
   when Daniel O'Connell he was alive.
   When Daniel O'Connell he was alive
   to work upon the railway, the railway.
   I'm weary of the railway,
   poor Paddy works on the railway.

6. In eighteen hundred and forty-six
   I made my trade to carrying bricks.
   I made my trade to carrying bricks
   for working on the railway.
   I'm weary of the railway,
   poor Paddy works on the railway.

7. In eighteen hundred and forty-seven
   poor Paddy was thinking of going to Heaven.
   poor Paddy was thinking of going to Heaven,
   to work upon the railway, the railway.
   I'm weary of the railway,
   poor Paddy works on the railway.

Midnight on the stormy deep

T'was mid - night on the storm - y deep,
1 |3 |5 |3 1 2| 2| 1

my so - li - ta - - - - ry watch I'd keep.___
2| |3 4| |5_____ |5 6| |5 |3___

___ And I think of her I'd left be - hind,
1 1 1 1 1| 6| 4| 6| |5

and asked if she'd be true and kind.
|5 6| |3 |5 1 2| 2| 1

2. I never shall forget the day,
   that I was forced to go away.
   In silence there my head she'd rest,
   and press me to her loving breast.

3. Oh Willy don't go back to sea,
   there's other girls as good as me.
   But none can love you true as I,
   pray don't go where the bullets fly.

4. The deep, deep sea may us divide,
   and I may be some other's bride.
   But still my thoughts will sometimes stray,
   to thee when thou art far away.

5. I never have proved false to thee,
   the heart I gave was true as thine.
   But you have proved untrue to me,
   I can no longer call thee mine.

6. Then fare-thee-well I'd rather make,
   my home upon some icy lake.
   Where the southern sun refused to shine,
   then to trust a love so false as thine.

Swing low, sweet chariot

Swing low, sweet cha - ri - ot,___ com-in' for to car-ry me
6| 4| 6| 4| 4| 2| 1 4| 4| 4| 4| 6| 6| 1|

home, swing low, sweet cha - ri - ot,___ com-in' for to car-ry me
1| |2 1| 6| 1| 4| 4| 2| 1 4| 4| 4| 4| 6| 6| |5

home. 1.I looked o - ver Jor-dan and what did I see,___
4| 6| 1| 4| 2| 4| 4| 4| 4| 4| 4| 2| 1

com-in' for to car-ry me home. A band___ of an-gels
4| 4| 4| 4| 6| 6| 1| 1| 1| |2 1| 6| 6| 4|

look-in' af-ter me,___ com-in' for to car-ry me home.
4| 4| 4| 4| 2| 1 4| 4| 4| 4| 6| 6| |5 4|

2. If you get there before I do,
   comin' for to carry me home,
   tell all o' God's children that I'm comin' too,
   comin' for to carry me home.

3. I'm sometimes up, I'm sometimes down,
   comin' for to carry me home,
   but still my soul feels heavenly bound,
   comin' for to carry me home.

The first Noel

The____ first____ No - el the___ an - gel did
|3 2| 1 2| |3 4| |5 6| |7 1| |7 6|

say was to cer - tain poor shep - herds in fields as they
|5 6| |7 1| |7 6| |5 6| |7 1| |5 4|

lay; In___ fields____ as___ they lay,___ keep - ing their
|3 |3 2| 1 2| |3 4| |5 6| |7 1| |7 6|

sheep, on a cold win - ter's night___ that was___ so
|5 6| |7 1| |7 6| |5 6| |7 1| |5 4|

deep. No - el,_____ No - el, No - el, No -
|3 |3 2| 1 2| |3 4| |5 1| |7 6| 6|

el, born is the King___ of Is - ra - el!
|5 1| |7 6| |5 6| |7 1| |5 4| |3

2. They looked up and saw a star
   shining in the east beyond them far,
   and to the earth it gave great light,
   and so it continued both day and night.

3. And by the light of that same star,
   three wise men came from country far;
   To seek for a king was their intent,
   and to follow the star wherever it went.

4. This star drew nigh to the northwest,
   o'er Bethlehem it took it rest,
   and there it did both stop and stay
   right over the place where Jesus lay.

5. Then entered in those wise men three
   full reverently upon their knee,
   and offered there in his presence
   their gold, and myrrh, and frankincense.

6. Then let us all with one accord
   sing praises to our heavenly Lord;
   That hath made heaven and earth of naught,
   and with his blood mankind hath bought.

My Bonnie lies over the ocean

My Bon - nie lies o - ver the o - cean,   my
|5 3| |2 1| |2 1 6| |5 |3 |5

Bon - nie lies o - ver the sea,   my Bon - nie lies
3| |2 1| 1| |7 1| |2 |5 3| |2 1|

o - ver the o - cean,   please bring back my Bon - nie to
|2 1 6| |5 |3 |5   6| |2 1| |7 6| |7

me._____   Bring   back,   bring   back, oh, bring back my
1|_____ |5   1| 6| |2 1| |7 7| |7

Bon - nie to me, to me.   Bring   back,   bring
|7 6| |7 1| |2 3| |5   1| |6

back, oh, bring back my Bon - nie to me._____
|2 1| |7 7| |7 |7 6| |7 1|_____

2. Last night as I lay on my pillow,
   last night as I lay on my bed.
   Last night as I lay on my pillow,
   I dreamed that my Bonnie was dead.
   Bring back, bring back,
   bring back my Bonnie to me, to me.
   Bring back, bring back,
   bring back my Bonnie to me.

3. Oh blow ye the winds o'er the ocean,
   and blow ye the winds o'er the sea.
   Oh blow ye the winds o'er the ocean,
   and bring back my Bonnie to me.
   Bring back, bring back,
   bring back my Bonnie to me, to me.
   Bring back, bring back,
   bring back my Bonnie to me.

4. The winds have blown over the ocean,
   the winds have blown over the sea.
   The winds have blown over the ocean,
   and brought back my Bonnie to me.
   Bring back, bring back,
   bring back my Bonnie to me, to me.
   Bring back, bring back,
   bring back my Bonnie to me.

How to read music

On the following pages we've compiled the most important basics of music notation. Don't worry if this all sounds a bit greek to you–you don't need to know this to play the songs in this book. Instead, these pages are intended for those who want to delve into the basics of reading music.

The staff

The **staff** is used to write down music. The staff is a group of five horizontal lines and the four spaces between them. It is read from left to right. At the end of the line you jump to the beginning of the next line. Notes can be written on the lines or the spaces in between.

Notes

There are different kind of notes, but they have one thing in common: Every note has a **notehead**. Most notes also have a **stem** and some of them an additional **flag** or a **beam**.

Pitch

Notes are written on the staff. You can tell the pitch of a note by its position on the staff.
Notes from the third line on upwards have their stem pointing down. The stem of all other notes is pointing up.
Notes that are too low or high for the staff are notated on **ledger lines**. You can think of ledger lines as a kind of abridged note lines.

Note value

You can tell the note value (duration of the note) by its shape. The next smaller note duration is derived by dividing the note value by two. For example: A half note is half the length of a whole note and two half notes once again add up to a whole note.

Rests

Rests are signs telling you to pause (e.g. play nothing) for a given period of time. For every note value, there's a corresponding rest. Don't mistake the whole rest for the half rest as they look quite similar!

Tip: Groups of eighth notes are usually notated using a beam–they're far easier to read this way.

Clef

The clef tells you the position of a reference note used to determine the positions of all other notes. If you see a G-clef, you can simply count: one note up from G = A; one note down from G = F and so on (see below).

This is an **F-clef**, telling you the position of the note F: the note F is located on the second line (counting from top to bottom).

This is a **G-clef**. It is the most common clef and tells you the position of the note G: the note G is located on the second line (counting from bottom to top).

Note names

There are seven different note names: A, B, C, D, E, F, G. After the seventh note, the note names repeat: A, B, C, D, E, F, G etc. These seven notes are also called **natural notes** or **naturals**.

To the right you can see one of the reasons there are several clefs: depending on the instrument, using another clef minimizes the number of ledger lines, making for a better readable notation.

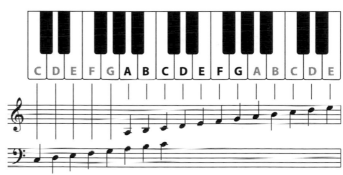

Accidentals

Take a look at the keyboard below. You'll see the note names you already know (white keys) but you'll also notice some new note names (the black keys). These new notes are created by raising or lowering one of the seven old notes.

Writing a ♯ (sharp) before a note raises it by a half-step. The note name is extended by an added "sharp" (e. g. G sharp).

G   G sharp

Writing a (flat) before a note lowers it by a half-step. The note name is extended by the word "flat" (e.g. G flat).

G   G flat

Here are all the notes on a piano keyboard– memorize them carefully!

There are two ways to name the notes of the black keys. For instance, the black key between F and G can either be called F sharp or G flat. Don't let this confuse you–it's the same pitch nevertheless!

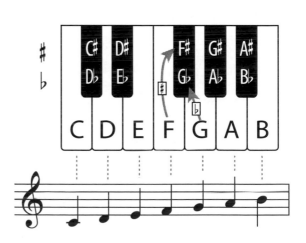

Key Signature

The **key signature** is a set of sharps (♯) or flats (♭) notated at the beginning of the staff immediately after the time signature. It designates notes that have to be played higher or lower than the corresponding natural notes. A sharp on a line or space raises all the notes on that line or space by a semitone. A flat on a line or space lowers all notes on that line or space by a semitone.

key signature

Bar (measure)

Notated music is divided into **bars** (or measures) by **bar lines**. The first note in every bar is accentuated slightly. The **time signature** at the beginning of the piece tells you how many notes make up a bar in this piece (here: 4 quarter notes). This time signature is called "Four-Four time". The end of a piece of music is indicated by a **final bar line**.

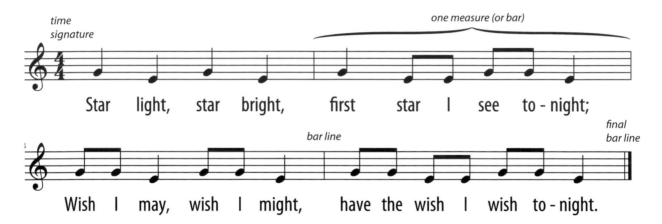

Time Signature

The time signature is notated at the beginning of the staff. It tells you how many beats each bar contains and which note value is equivalent to one beat. Here are some common time signatures and how to count them:

Ties and slurs

Two notes of the same pitch can be connected by a curved line, the **tie**. The second note is not played separately. Instead, its duration is simply added to the duration of the first note (e.g. two tied quarter notes have the same duration as a half note).

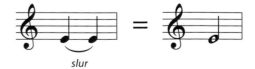

slur

There's another musical sign looking very similar to the tie, the **slur**. Two or more notes connected by a slur are meant to be played independently, but seamlessly after another (also called legato playing). The distinction between the tie and the slur is easy, however. While the tie connects notes of the **same pitch and name**, the slur is only used on notes of **different pitches and names**.

Dotted notes

A dot behind a note increases the duration of that note by half its original length. This sounds much more complicated than it actually is:

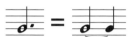

A dotted half note has the duration of a half note plus a quarter note.

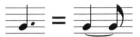

A dotted quarter note has the duration of a quarter note plus as eighth note.

Triplets

Dividing a note value by three instead of two is called a triplet. This sounds way more complicated than it actually is. Have a look at the graphic to the right. In standard notation, triplets are notated by the number "3" and often grouped with a small bracket.

A common way to count triplets is: "1-and-e, 2-and-e"

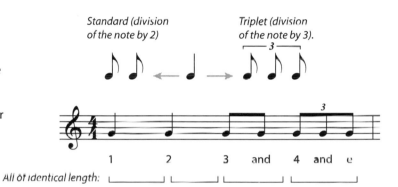

Repeat signs

tell you to repeat parts of a piece of music (or even the whole piece).

Here the whole song is played twice: 1 2 3 4 5 6 / 8 **1 2 3 4 5 6 7 8**

Measures 3 and 4 are repeated once: 1 2 3 4 **3 4** 5 6 7 8

Repeat with first and second ending (or volta brackets): 1 2 3 4 5 6 **1 2 3 4** 7 8

Instrument labels

Choose the sticker that fits your instrument and fix it to the top of your kalimba using a strip of clear adhesive tape.

Photocopy this page so your book remains complete.

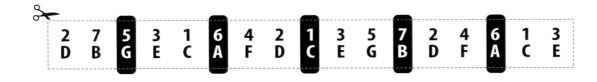

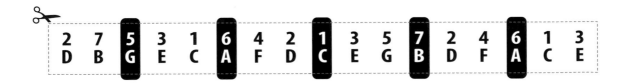

Made in United States
North Haven, CT
28 October 2022

26022139R00043